THE NEW MAYO CLINIC DIET
FOR EASY WEIGHT LOSS

Transform Your Body and Lose Weight with

100+ Tasty, Easy, Budget-friendly recipes

Ashley Brooke M.D.

COPYRIGHT PAGE

and solutions provided here may not apply to your unique situation. Lost earnings, lost money, missed chances, and other comparable outcomes are not considered economic losses for which the publisher or author can be held accountable. It is important to remember that the electronic versions may exclude certain information that appeared in the print versions.

TABLE OF CONTENTS

PART 1: INTRODUCTION

The Mayo Clinic is a non-profit institution that provides medical treatment, conducts medical research, and provides health education, and they have created a weight loss regimen called the Mayo Clinic Diet. This eating plan is designed to aid in long-term, healthy weight loss, rather than the short-term weight loss typically seen with fad diets.

The goal of the Mayo Clinic Diet is to empower people to take control of their health by improving their diet and exercise routines. It promotes eating meals from all the different food categories to get the right mix of nutrients.

The notion of energy balance is central to the Mayo Clinic Diet. This indicates that one's calorie intake should be equal to one's calorie expenditure. Losing weight should be done slowly and carefully, and this may be accomplished by creating a calorie deficit. The approach does not advocate for severe calorie restriction or deprivation, however, since it stresses the significance of weight reduction that is both long-lasting and healthful.

Making better meal selections is a central tenet of the Mayo Clinic Diet. It recommends that people eat more plant-based foods, as well as whole grains, lean meats, and healthy fats. These meals are low in calories yet high in beneficial nutrients like fiber and vitamins.

Sugary drinks, processed meals, and foods high in saturated fat and added sugars are discouraged on the diet in order to facilitate weight reduction. It stresses the need of paying attention to one's hunger and fullness cues and practicing portion management and mindful eating.

The Mayo Clinic Diet is a set of dietary guidelines that also emphasizes the need of regular physical exercise. Cardiovascular and strength training are only two of the types of exercise that are recommended and explained so that they may be incorporated into daily life.

The Mayo Clinic Diet stands out due to its two-pronged strategy. The "Lose It!" phase is a two-week kickstart designed to get you on the path to weight reduction and healthy behaviors for good. The program encourages participants to adopt a more healthful diet and increase their levels of physical exercise. The "Live It!" phase is the next step, and it's a long-term maintenance phase that offers advice for keeping the weight off permanently.

Professionals such as doctors, dietitians, and psychologists are there to help you every step of the way on the Mayo Clinic Diet. The diet also stresses the value of obtaining social support, keeping track of one's progress, and establishing reasonable objectives.

The Mayo Clinic Diet is an all-encompassing plan for slimming down and improving one's health that is supported by scientific research. It's an approach that can help people attain and maintain a healthy weight since it emphasizes eating well, limiting one's portion sizes, getting regular exercise, and altering one's habits over the long haul.

What is The Mayo Clinic Diet

It is a long-term, sustainable improvements in food and exercise are emphasized rather than short-term fads or crash diets.

Instead than cutting out or severely limiting certain food categories, the Mayo Clinic Diet encourages a well-rounded and healthy diet. Fruits, vegetables, whole grains, lean proteins, and healthy fats are encouraged, but additional sweets and saturated fats are restricted. It promotes thoughtful eating and smaller portions, as well as the consumption of nutrient-dense meals that leave you feeling full while keeping your calorie intake low.

There are two parts to the program:

Lose It!: The goal of this first, two-week period is to set the tone for sustained weight reduction success. Altering one's diet means switching to healthier options. Healthy eating, appropriate portion sizes, and regular exercise are all topics that will be covered at this stage.

Live It!: This stage is a permanent way of thinking about one's weight and health. It will help you develop healthy diet and exercise routines that will last a lifetime. It stresses the need of developing lifelong positive routines, establishing attainable objectives, and surrounding oneself with encouraging people.

The Mayo Clinic Diet recognizes the importance of exercise for both weight control and general well-being. Walking and cycling are only two examples of the aerobic workouts that are advocated with strength training to increase muscle mass and speed up the body's metabolic rate.

The Mayo Clinic Diet is not to be confused with the Mayo Clinic's recommended diet for treating a variety of medical issues. To make sure a weight reduction or diet plan is safe and effective for you, a healthcare provider or qualified dietitian should be consulted first.

The Origin of The Mayo Clinic Diet

The Mayo Clinic Diet originated from the prestigious Mayo Clinic, a renowned medical institution located in Rochester, Minnesota. The clinic has been at the forefront of medical education, research, and patient care for well over a century.

The Mayo Clinic Diet was created by a group of medical professionals, including doctors, nutritionists, and dietitians. A complete and evidence-based weight reduction program was developed by the team, drawing on their collective expertise in nutrition and weight management.

The diet may be traced back to the Mayo Clinic's dedication to integrative medicine and individualized treatment plans. The clinic's goal was to develop a weight loss program that also enhanced patients' health and quality of life by addressing the known link between nutrition and health.

The Mayo Clinic Diet is an approach to weight loss that avoids the common flaws that plague other diet plans. Its goal is to help people lose weight in a healthy way that can be maintained over time, rather than via drastic measures like starvation or excessive exercise.

The Mayo Clinic team made sure the therapy was successful and safe by doing considerable study and analyzing scientific data. They included the most recent nutritional standards and recommendations and stressed the value of evidence-based approaches.

The Mayo Clinic's dedication to personalised treatment is reflected in its dietary recommendations. It takes into account the fact that people vary greatly in terms of their requirements, preferences, and health status. The program allows for a more individualized and successful weight reduction journey by providing individualized meal plans, recipes, and assistance.

In conclusion, the Mayo Clinic Diet was developed out of the clinic's dedication to provide high-quality, evidence-based medical treatment. It was created by professionals to overcome the problems encountered by previous diet plans. The Mayo Clinic Diet is a reliable and useful strategy for people who want to lose weight and improve their health because of its emphasis on long-term lifestyle changes, evidence-based practices, and individualized approach.

Benefit of The Mayo Clinic Diet

The Mayo Clinic Diet is a systematic, scientific method for achieving your weight reduction and health improvement goals. Unlike fad diets and fast solutions, this program from the highly regarded Mayo Clinic focuses on making permanent improvements to one's way of life. The approach is grounded in scientific data, using the knowledge of doctors and dietitians.

By emphasizing good nutrition, portion management, and regular exercise, it encourages safe, long-term weight loss. A healthy and well-rounded diet ensures that people get all the nutrients they need while also decreasing their consumption of processed and harmful foods.

The Mayo Clinic Diet also includes a section on changing your behaviors, with advice on how to deal with emotional eating and methods for creating new, healthy routines that will last. It acknowledges the need of treating psychological and behavioral components of weight reduction in addition to food modifications.

The program not only helps you lose weight, but it also improves your health in many other ways, such as by lowering your cholesterol, reducing your risk of chronic illnesses, and giving you more energy. By making positive lifestyle changes, people can enhance their health and happiness.

The Mayo Clinic Diet is individualized to suit each person's needs and tastes, as well as their current state of health. Because it takes into account the specifics of each person's situation, personalization improves the odds of success and adherence.

When it comes to long-term success with weight reduction and increased health, the Mayo Clinic Diet is a reliable and successful regimen. Achieving and maintaining a healthy weight and way of life can be aided by this program because of its individualized nature, emphasis on sustainable lifestyle changes, emphasis on a balanced and nutritious diet, emphasis on behavior modification tactics, and health advantages beyond weight reduction.

PART 2: GETTING STARTED ON THE MAYO CLINIC DIET

Starting The Mayo Clinic Diet is easy and just requires a few basic measures. These measures are meant to assist people in making the change to a healthy lifestyle and laying the groundwork for long-term weight loss and better health.

First and foremost, you must have a firm grasp of the tenets and regulations of The Mayo Clinic Diet. This may be done by consulting authoritative books or online resources that explain the software in depth. Get comfortable with the diet's fundamental ideas, including as its push for moderation in all things, a focus on healthy foods, and the need of regular exercise.

The next step is to take stock of your existing diet and make note of the areas where improvement is needed. Think about what you consume on a regular basis and how much you eat. By examining your own habits and preferences, you may determine where changes are needed and what kind of progress is actually possible.

Making a plan is the next step after becoming educated about the diet and taking stock of your eating habits. Achievable targets for weight loss and health enhancement are essential. Talking to a qualified medical expert, like a certified dietician, can help you develop a strategy that works for your specific situation.

The Mayo Clinic Diet emphasizes the importance of eating a healthy, well-rounded diet. This eating plan restricts processed meals, sugary snacks, and high-calorie beverages in favor of nutritious foods such fruits, vegetables, whole grains, lean proteins, and healthy fats. Create a menu centered around nutrient-dense foods you love eating by making a list of your favorites.

The Mayo Clinic Diet emphasizes both healthy food and exercise as essential components. Include regular exercise in your schedule; ideally, you'll do some cardio, some weight training, and some stretching. Pick some things you already like doing and work up to doing them for longer and harder.

Finally, it's crucial to monitor your development and make changes as required. Maintaining a food diary is a great method to keep track of what you're eating and to reflect on your progress or setbacks. Check in on your progress toward your targets frequently, and make course corrections as needed.

Keep in mind that the Mayo Clinic Diet is not a quick remedy, but rather a way of life. Don't give up, take things slowly, and if you need to, go to a doctor or join a support group. If you give The Mayo Clinic Diet your complete attention and effort, you will see positive results that will endure for a lifetime.

Recommended Food on The Mayo Clinic Diet

To aid with weight reduction and general health, the Mayo Clinic Diet suggests eating a wide range of full, nutrient-rich foods. Some examples of food categories and items that should be included in the diet are as follows:

The high nutritional content and low calorie density of fruits and vegetables make them crucial parts of The Mayo Clinic Diet. Berrys, leafy greens, citrus fruits, cruciferous vegetables, and many more should all find a place in your daily diet. They taste great raw, cooked, or blended into a healthy smoothie or salad.

Whole grains are a good source of sustained energy since they include fiber, vitamins, and minerals. Brown rice, quinoa, whole wheat bread, oats, and whole wheat pasta are all excellent examples of whole grains that you should include in your diet.

Choose protein sources that are low in saturated fat, such as lean meats. These might range from eggs and Greek yogurt to skinless chicken and seafood. These protein foods aid in muscle maintenance by supplying necessary amino acids.

Olive oil, avocados, almonds, and seeds are all examples of healthy fats that should be used in moderation. These aid in satiation, promote nutritional absorption, and are good for your heart.

Skip the whole milk and go for skim milk, fat-free yogurt, and reduced-fat cheese instead. These are low in saturated fat and include calcium and protein.

Drink enough of water throughout the day to maintain a healthy level of hydration in your body. Reduce or eliminate your consumption of sugary drinks and replace them with water, herbal tea, or infused water.

Even while we should prioritize eating complete, nutrient-dense meals, we still need to watch our portions and eat consciously. The Mayo Clinic Diet stresses moderation and awareness in eating to keep things under check.

It is important to note that The Mayo Clinic Diet also includes individualized meal planning and recipes. The information and ideas presented here may be helpful as you seek to improve your diet by include more of the items that are suggested.

If you want specific advice and assurance that you're getting enough nutrients on The Mayo Clinic Diet, talking to a dietitian or other healthcare expert is a must.

Foods to Stay Away from on The Mayo Clinic Diet

Calorie-dense, unhealthy-fat-containing, added-sugar- and sodium-laden foods are strongly discouraged by the Mayo Clinic Diet. On The Mayo Clinic Diet, these items are generally avoided or taken in moderation.

Sausage, hot dogs, and bacon are just a few examples of processed meats that are often rich in harmful fats and salt. They've been linked to an uptick in the incidence of chronic illness. Meats with high levels of saturated fat and calories, such as fatty cuts of beef or pork, should be eaten in moderation.

Limit your consumption of sugary snacks and sweets like candy, cookies, cakes, pastries, and sugary drinks. They contribute to weight gain and general unhealthiness because of the empty calories they supply.

Calorie-dense and nutrient-poor are common characteristics of highly processed foods like packaged snacks, chips, sugary cereals, and fast food. They often have unhealthy amounts of salt, sodium, and added sugars. Avoiding excessive use of these products is recommended.

White bread, white rice, and refined pasta are examples of refined grains. During processing, the bran and germ are removed from these products, reducing the dietary fiber and nutritional value.

Instead, whole grains are advocated on the Mayo Clinic Diet.

Soda, fruit juices with added sugars, energy drinks, and sweetened coffees and teas are all examples of sugary beverages that are high in calories and sugar. These beverages have been linked to weight gain and negative health effects.

High-sodium diets are linked to hypertension and other health problems, so it's important to watch what you eat in this category. Processed meats, canned soup, packaged snacks, and some condiments are all examples of foods that are high in sodium.

The Mayo Clinic Diet may recommend cutting back or eliminating these foods, but remember that moderation and balance are still essential. The diet encourages sustainable behavioral changes over short-term restriction and permits moderate overeating on occasion.

Working with a registered dietitian or healthcare professional to receive individualized guidance and support in making healthier food choices and managing one's unique dietary needs is highly recommended for those following The Mayo Clinic Diet.

PART 3: 30 DAYS MAYO CLINIC DIET RECIPES

BREAKFAST RECIPES FOR WEIGHT LOSS

Greek yogurt with fresh berries and a sprinkle of nuts:

Ingredients

1 cup Greek yogurt

Assorted fresh berries (e.g., strawberries, blueberries, raspberries)

Mixed nuts (e.g., almonds, walnuts)

Instructions

In a bowl, add the Greek yogurt.

Wash the berries and add them to the bowl.

Sprinkle a handful of mixed nuts on top.

Mix gently and enjoy!

Veggie omelet made with egg whites, spinach, bell peppers, and mushrooms:

Ingredients

3 egg whites

Handful of fresh spinach leaves

1/4 cup sliced bell peppers

1/4 cup sliced mushrooms

Salt and pepper to taste

Cooking spray or a small amount of olive oil

Instructions

Heat a non-stick skillet over medium heat and coat it with cooking spray or a small amount of olive oil.

Add the sliced bell peppers and mushrooms to the skillet and cook until they soften.

In a separate bowl, whisk the egg whites with salt and pepper.

Pour the egg whites into the skillet over the vegetables.

Cook until the omelet is set, flipping it once to ensure even cooking.

Slide the omelet onto a plate and fold it in half.

Serve hot.

Whole grain toast topped with avocado and sliced tomatoes:

Ingredients

2 slices of whole grain bread

1 ripe avocado

1 tomato, sliced

Salt and pepper to taste

Instructions

Toast the slices of whole grain bread until they are golden brown.

Cut the ripe avocado in half, remove the pit, and scoop out the flesh.

Mash the avocado with a fork until it reaches your desired consistency.

Spread the mashed avocado evenly on the toast slices.

Place the sliced tomatoes on top.

Season with salt and pepper.

Enjoy!

Oatmeal cooked with water or skim milk, topped with sliced bananas and a drizzle of honey:

Ingredients

1/2 cup rolled oats

1 cup water or skim milk

1 ripe banana, sliced

1 teaspoon honey

Instructions

In a saucepan, bring the water or skim milk to a boil.

Stir in the rolled oats and reduce the heat to low.

Cook the oats for about 5 minutes, stirring occasionally, until they reach your desired consistency.

Remove the saucepan from heat and transfer the oatmeal to a bowl.

Top with sliced bananas.

Drizzle with honey.

Stir gently and enjoy while warm.

Whole grain cereal with skim milk and a side of fresh fruit:

Ingredients

1 cup whole grain cereal (such as bran flakes, whole wheat flakes, or oats)

1 cup skim milk

Assorted fresh fruit (e.g., berries, sliced bananas, sliced peaches)

Instructions

Pour the whole grain cereal into a bowl.

Add skim milk over the cereal.

Slice the fresh fruit and place it alongside the cereal.

Mix the cereal and milk, and enjoy it with bites of fresh fruit.

Cottage cheese with sliced peaches and a sprinkle of cinnamon:

Ingredients

1/2 cup cottage cheese

1 ripe peach, sliced

A sprinkle of cinnamon

Instructions

Place the cottage cheese in a bowl.

Add the sliced peaches on top.

Sprinkle cinnamon over the peaches and cottage cheese.

Mix gently and enjoy.

Quinoa breakfast bowl with mixed berries, almond milk, and a dash of cinnamon:

Ingredients

1/2 cup cooked quinoa

Assorted mixed berries (e.g., strawberries, blueberries, raspberries)

1/2 cup almond milk (unsweetened)

A dash of cinnamon

Instructions

In a bowl, combine cooked quinoa and mixed berries.

Pour almond milk over the quinoa and berries.

Sprinkle a dash of cinnamon on top.

Stir gently and enjoy.

Smoked salmon on a whole wheat bagel with cream cheese and cucumber slices:

Ingredients

1 whole wheat bagel

2 ounces smoked salmon

2 tablespoons cream cheese (low-fat)

Cucumber slices

Instructions

Slice the whole wheat bagel in half.

Spread cream cheese on each bagel half.

Lay smoked salmon slices on top of the cream cheese.

Add cucumber slices on the salmon.

Sandwich the bagel halves together.

Enjoy!

Spinach and mushroom frittata made with egg whites:

Ingredients

1 cup egg whites

Handful of fresh spinach leaves

1/4 cup sliced mushrooms

Salt and pepper to taste

Cooking spray or a small amount of olive oil

Instructions

Preheat the oven to 350°F (175°C).

In a bowl, whisk the egg whites with salt and pepper.

Heat an oven-safe skillet over medium heat and coat it with cooking spray or a small amount of olive oil.

Add the sliced mushrooms to the skillet and cook until they soften.

Add the fresh spinach leaves to the skillet and cook until wilted.

Pour the whisked egg whites over the vegetables in the skillet.

Transfer the skillet to the preheated oven and bake for about 15-20 minutes, until the frittata is set.

Remove from the oven and let it cool slightly before slicing and serving.

Homemade smoothie with spinach, banana, almond milk, and a scoop of protein powder:

Ingredients

Handful of fresh spinach leaves

1 ripe banana

1 cup almond milk (unsweetened)

1 scoop of protein powder (flavor of your choice)

Instructions

Place the fresh spinach leaves, ripe banana, almond milk, and protein powder in a blender.

Blend until smooth and well combined.

Pour into a glass and enjoy the refreshing smoothie.

Whole grain pancakes topped with Greek yogurt and fresh fruit:

Ingredients

1 cup whole wheat flour

1 tablespoon honey or maple syrup

1 teaspoon baking powder

1/2 teaspoon baking soda

1 cup buttermilk or almond milk

1 large egg

Cooking spray or a small amount of oil

Greek yogurt

Assorted fresh fruit for topping (e.g., sliced strawberries, blueberries, raspberries)

Instructions

In a mixing bowl, combine the whole wheat flour, honey or maple syrup, baking powder, and baking soda.

In a separate bowl, whisk together the buttermilk or almond milk and egg.

Gradually pour the wet ingredients into the dry ingredients, stirring until just combined.

Heat a non-stick skillet or griddle over medium heat and coat it with cooking spray or a small amount of oil.

Pour 1/4 cup of the pancake batter onto the skillet for each pancake.

Cook until bubbles form on the surface, then flip and cook the other side until golden brown.

Repeat with the remaining batter.

Top the pancakes with a dollop of Greek yogurt and fresh fruit.

Serve warm.

Breakfast burrito with scrambled egg whites, black beans, diced tomatoes, and salsa:

Ingredients

3 egg whites

1/4 cup canned black beans, rinsed and drained

1 small tomato, diced

2 whole wheat tortillas

Salsa for topping

Instructions

In a non-stick skillet, scramble the egg whites over medium heat until cooked through.

Warm the black beans in a separate pan or in the microwave.

Divide the scrambled egg whites, black beans, and diced tomatoes evenly between the two whole wheat tortillas.

Roll up the tortillas into burritos.

Serve with salsa for topping.

Chia seed pudding made with almond milk, topped with sliced almonds and blueberries:

Ingredients

3 tablespoons chia seeds

1 cup almond milk (unsweetened)

1 tablespoon honey or maple syrup (optional)

Sliced almonds

Fresh blueberries

Instructions

In a bowl, combine the chia seeds and almond milk.

Stir well to ensure the chia seeds are evenly distributed and not clumped together.

If desired, sweeten the mixture with honey or maple syrup.

Cover the bowl and refrigerate overnight or for at least 4 hours until the chia seeds absorb the liquid and form a pudding-like consistency.

Before serving, give the chia seed pudding a good stir.

Top with sliced almonds and fresh blueberries.

Enjoy chilled.

Whole grain English muffin with lean turkey breast and a slice of low-fat cheese:

Ingredients

1 whole grain English muffin, split

2-3 ounces lean turkey breast

1 slice low-fat cheese (e.g., Swiss, cheddar)

Instructions

Toast the whole grain English muffin until golden brown.

Layer the lean turkey breast on one half of the toasted English muffin.

Place the slice of low-fat cheese on top of the turkey.

Close the sandwich with the other half of the English muffin.

Optionally, warm the sandwich in a toaster oven or microwave until the cheese melts.

Serve warm.

Vegetable and quinoa breakfast muffins:

Ingredients

1 cup cooked quinoa

1/2 cup grated zucchini

1/4 cup diced bell peppers

2 green onions, finely chopped

1/4 cup grated Parmesan cheese

2 large eggs

Salt and pepper to taste

Cooking spray

Instructions

Preheat the oven to 375°F (190°C) and grease a muffin tin with cooking spray.

In a mixing bowl, combine the cooked quinoa, grated zucchini, diced bell peppers, green onions, Parmesan cheese, eggs, salt, and pepper.

Mix well until all ingredients are evenly incorporated.

Spoon the mixture into the greased muffin tin, filling each cup about three-quarters full.

Bake for 20-25 minutes or until the tops are golden brown and the muffins are set.

Remove from the oven and allow them to cool for a few minutes.

Gently remove the muffins from the tin and serve warm or at room temperature.

Peanut butter and banana wrap in a whole wheat tortilla:

Ingredients

1 whole wheat tortilla

2 tablespoons peanut butter (natural, no added sugar)

1 ripe banana

Instructions

Spread peanut butter evenly on the whole wheat tortilla.

Peel the ripe banana and place it in the center of the tortilla.

Roll up the tortilla, enclosing the banana.

Slice the wrap in half or into smaller portions, if desired.

Enjoy as a handheld breakfast option.

Scrambled tofu with mixed vegetables and a side of whole grain toast:

Ingredients

1/2 block of firm tofu, crumbled

Assorted mixed vegetables (e.g., bell peppers, onions, spinach)

Salt, pepper, and turmeric to taste

Cooking spray or a small amount of oil

1-2 slices of whole grain toast

Instructions

Heat a non-stick skillet over medium heat and coat it with cooking spray or a small amount of oil.

Add the crumbled tofu to the skillet and cook for a few minutes until slightly browned.

Add the mixed vegetables to the skillet and sauté until tender.

Season with salt, pepper, and turmeric to taste.

Serve the scrambled tofu and vegetables with a side of whole grain toast.

Low-fat cottage cheese mixed with diced pineapple and a sprinkle of cinnamon:

Ingredients

1/2 cup low-fat cottage cheese

1/4 cup diced pineapple

A sprinkle of cinnamon

Instructions

In a bowl, combine the low-fat cottage cheese and diced pineapple.

Sprinkle cinnamon on top.

Mix gently and enjoy.

Whole grain waffle topped with a dollop of Greek yogurt and fresh strawberries:

Ingredients

1 whole grain waffle (store-bought or homemade)

Greek yogurt

Fresh strawberries, sliced

Instructions

Toast the whole grain waffle until it is crisp and golden.

Place the waffle on a plate.

Add a dollop of Greek yogurt on top of the waffle.

Arrange sliced fresh strawberries on the yogurt.

Enjoy the delicious waffle with a healthy twist.

Vegetable and turkey sausage breakfast casserole:

Ingredients

4 turkey sausage links, sliced

1/2 cup diced bell peppers

1/2 cup diced onions

1 cup chopped spinach

6 large eggs

1/2 cup milk (skim or low-fat)

Salt and pepper to taste

Cooking spray

Instructions

Preheat the oven to 375°F (190°C) and grease a baking dish with cooking spray.

In a skillet, cook the turkey sausage slices until browned.

Add the diced bell peppers and onions to the skillet and cook until they soften.

Add the chopped spinach to the skillet and cook until wilted.

In a separate bowl, whisk together the eggs, milk, salt, and pepper.

Spread the cooked sausage, vegetables, and spinach evenly in the greased baking dish.

Pour the egg mixture over the sausage and vegetables.

Bake for approximately 25-30 minutes or until the eggs are set and the top is golden brown.

Remove from the oven and allow it to cool slightly before serving.

LUNCH RECIPES FOR WEIGHT LOSS

Grilled Chicken Breast Salad:

Ingredients

4 ounces (113 grams) grilled chicken breast

2 cups mixed greens

2 tablespoons balsamic vinaigrette dressing

Instructions

Season the chicken breast with salt and pepper, then grill it until cooked through.

Slice the grilled chicken into thin strips.

In a large bowl, combine the mixed greens.

Add the sliced grilled chicken on top of the greens.

Drizzle the balsamic vinaigrette dressing over the salad.

Toss gently to coat the salad evenly.

Serve and enjoy!

Turkey Wrap:

Ingredients

1 whole wheat tortilla

3 ounces (85 grams) lean turkey breast

Lettuce leaves

Tomato slices

Mustard (to taste)

Instructions

Lay the whole wheat tortilla flat on a clean surface.

Spread mustard over the tortilla.

Place the lettuce leaves on top of the mustard.

Layer the turkey breast slices on the lettuce.

Add tomato slices on top of the turkey.

Roll the tortilla tightly, tucking in the ingredients as you go.

Slice the wrap in half diagonally.

Serve and enjoy!

Quinoa Salad:

Ingredients

1 cup cooked quinoa

1 cup diced cucumbers

1 cup diced bell peppers

½ cup cherry tomatoes, halved

2 tablespoons chopped fresh herbs (such as parsley or basil)

2 tablespoons lemon juice

1 tablespoon olive oil

Salt and pepper to taste

Instructions

In a large bowl, combine the cooked quinoa, diced cucumbers, bell peppers, cherry tomatoes, and fresh herbs.

In a separate small bowl, whisk together the lemon juice, olive oil, salt, and pepper.

Pour the dressing over the quinoa mixture.

Toss gently to coat the ingredients evenly.

Taste and adjust seasoning if needed.

Serve chilled and enjoy!

Steamed Salmon with Roasted Asparagus:

Ingredients

4 ounces (113 grams) salmon fillet

½ bunch asparagus spears

1 teaspoon olive oil

Salt and pepper to taste

½ cup cooked brown rice

Instructions

Preheat the oven to 400°F (200°C).

Place the salmon fillet on a baking sheet lined with parchment paper.

Drizzle the salmon with olive oil and season with salt and pepper.

Place the asparagus spears on the same baking sheet.

Drizzle the asparagus with olive oil and season with salt and pepper.

Roast the salmon and asparagus in the preheated oven for about 12-15 minutes or until the salmon is cooked through and the asparagus is tender.

Serve the salmon and asparagus with a side of cooked brown rice.

Enjoy!

Veggie Stir-Fry:

Ingredients

4 ounces (113 grams) tofu, cubed

1 cup broccoli florets

1 carrot, sliced

½ cup snow peas

1 clove garlic, minced

1 tablespoon low-sodium soy sauce

1 teaspoon sesame oil

½ cup cooked brown rice

Instructions

Heat the sesame oil in a large skillet or wok over medium-high heat.

Add the tofu cubes and cook until golden brown on all sides.

Remove the tofu from the skillet and set it aside.

In the same skillet, add the minced garlic and cook for about 30 seconds.

Add the broccoli florets, carrot slices, and snow peas to the skillet.

Stir-fry the vegetables for about 3-4 minutes or until they are tender-crisp.

Return the tofu to the skillet and add the low-sodium soy sauce.

Cook for an additional minute, stirring to coat the tofu and vegetables with the sauce.

Serve the stir-fry over cooked brown rice.

Enjoy!

Spinach and Feta Omelet:

Ingredients

2 large eggs

½ cup fresh spinach leaves

2 tablespoons crumbled feta cheese

Salt and pepper to taste

Fresh fruit for serving

Instructions

In a bowl, beat the eggs until well combined.

Heat a non-stick skillet over medium heat.

Add the beaten eggs to the skillet and swirl to cover the bottom.

Cook the eggs for 2-3 minutes or until they start to set.

Sprinkle the spinach leaves and feta cheese evenly over half of the omelet.

Fold the other half of the omelet over the filling.

Cook for an additional 1-2 minutes or until the cheese is melted and the omelet is cooked through.

Season with salt and pepper to taste.

Serve the omelet with fresh fruit on the side.

Enjoy!

Black Bean and Corn Salad:

Ingredients

1 cup canned black beans, rinsed and drained

1 cup corn kernels

½ cup diced tomatoes

½ avocado, diced

2 tablespoons chopped fresh cilantro

Juice of 1 lime

Salt and pepper to taste

Instructions

In a large bowl, combine the black beans, corn kernels, diced tomatoes, diced avocado, and chopped cilantro.

Squeeze the lime juice over the salad.

Season with salt and pepper to taste.

Toss gently to combine all the ingredients.

Taste and adjust seasoning if needed.

Serve chilled and enjoy!

Greek Yogurt with Fresh Berries:

Ingredients

1 cup plain Greek yogurt

½ cup fresh berries (such as strawberries, blueberries, or raspberries)

1 tablespoon sliced almonds

1 teaspoon honey (optional)

Instructions

In a bowl, spoon the Greek yogurt.

Top the yogurt with fresh berries and sliced almonds.

Drizzle with honey if desired.

Mix gently to combine the ingredients.

Serve and enjoy!

Lentil Soup:

Ingredients

1 cup cooked lentils

2 cups low-sodium vegetable broth

½ cup diced carrots

½ cup diced celery

½ cup diced onion

1 clove garlic, minced

1 teaspoon olive oil

½ teaspoon dried thyme

Salt and pepper to taste

Instructions

Heat the olive oil in a large pot over medium heat.

Add the minced garlic, diced onion, diced carrots, and diced celery to the pot.

Sauté the vegetables for about 5 minutes or until they are softened.

Add the cooked lentils, vegetable broth, dried thyme, salt, and pepper to the pot.

Bring the soup to a boil, then reduce the heat to low and simmer for about 15-20 minutes.

Taste and adjust seasoning if needed.

Serve the lentil soup hot.

Enjoy!

Grilled Shrimp Skewers:

Ingredients

4 ounces (113 grams) shrimp, peeled and deveined

1 small zucchini, sliced

1 small bell pepper, cut into chunks

1 teaspoon olive oil

Salt and pepper to taste

½ cup cooked quinoa

Instructions

Preheat a grill or grill pan over medium-high heat.

Thread the shrimp, zucchini slices, and bell pepper chunks onto skewers.

Drizzle the skewers with olive oil and season with salt and pepper.

Grill the skewers for about 3-4 minutes per side or until the shrimp are cooked through.

Remove the skewers from the grill and let them cool slightly.

Serve the grilled shrimp skewers with a side of cooked quinoa.

Enjoy!

Caprese Salad:

Ingredients

1 large tomato, sliced

4 ounces (113 grams) fresh mozzarella cheese, sliced

Fresh basil leaves

Balsamic glaze

Salt and pepper to taste

Instructions

Arrange the tomato slices and fresh mozzarella slices on a plate.

Tuck fresh basil leaves between the tomato and mozzarella slices.

Drizzle the salad with balsamic glaze.

Season with salt and pepper to taste.

Serve the Caprese salad immediately.

Enjoy!

Whole Wheat Pita with Hummus:

Ingredients

1 whole wheat pita bread

2 tablespoons hummus

Sliced cucumbers

Roasted red peppers

Instructions

Cut the whole wheat pita bread in half to create two pockets.

Spread 1 tablespoon of hummus inside each pita pocket.

Stuff the pita pockets with sliced cucumbers and roasted red peppers.

Serve the whole wheat pita with hummus.

Enjoy!

Tuna Salad Sandwich:

Ingredients

1 can tuna, drained

2 tablespoons Greek yogurt

1 stalk celery, finely chopped

2 tablespoons red onion, finely chopped

Salt and pepper to taste

Whole wheat bread

Instructions

In a bowl, combine the drained tuna, Greek yogurt, celery, and red onion.

Mix well to combine all the ingredients.

Season with salt and pepper to taste.

Spread the tuna salad mixture onto whole wheat bread slices.

Assemble the sandwich and cut in half if desired.

Serve the tuna salad sandwich.

Enjoy!

Roasted Vegetable and Quinoa Wrap:

Ingredients

1 cup mixed roasted vegetables (such as bell peppers, zucchini, and eggplant)

½ cup cooked quinoa

2 tablespoons hummus

Whole wheat wrap or tortilla

Instructions

Warm the whole wheat wrap or tortilla.

Spread hummus evenly on the wrap.

Layer the roasted vegetables and cooked quinoa on top of the hummus.

Roll the wrap tightly, tucking in the ingredients as you go.

Slice the wrap in half diagonally if desired.

Serve the roasted vegetable and quinoa wrap.

Enjoy!

Steamed Edamame with Raw Veggies:

Ingredients

1 cup steamed edamame

Sea salt to taste

Carrot sticks

Celery sticks

Instructions

Steam the edamame according to package instructions.

Sprinkle the steamed edamame with sea salt.

Serve the edamame with carrot and celery sticks.

Enjoy!

Grilled Chicken or Turkey Burger Lettuce Wraps:

Ingredients

4 ounces (113 grams) grilled chicken or turkey burger patty

Lettuce leaves

Sliced tomatoes

Sliced onions

Instructions

Grill the chicken or turkey burger patty until cooked through.

Place the cooked patty on a lettuce leaf.

Top with sliced tomatoes and onions.

Wrap the lettuce leaf around the patty and toppings to create a lettuce wrap.

Repeat for the remaining patties.

Serve the grilled chicken or turkey burger lettuce wraps.

Enjoy!

Mexican-Inspired Quinoa Bowl:

Ingredients

½ cup cooked quinoa

½ cup canned black beans, rinsed and drained

½ cup corn kernels

½ cup diced tomatoes

1 tablespoon fresh lime juice

1 tablespoon chopped fresh cilantro

Salt and pepper to taste

Instructions

In a bowl, combine the cooked quinoa, black beans, corn kernels, diced tomatoes, lime juice, and chopped cilantro.

Season with salt and pepper to taste.

Mix well to combine all the ingredients.

Serve the Mexican-inspired quinoa bowl.

Enjoy!

Asian-Inspired Chicken Lettuce Wraps:

Ingredients

4 ounces (113 grams) grilled chicken breast, diced

Lettuce leaves

¼ cup shredded carrots

¼ cup chopped cucumber

2 tablespoons low-sodium soy sauce

1 tablespoon rice vinegar

1 teaspoon sesame oil

1 teaspoon honey

1 teaspoon grated ginger

Sesame seeds for garnish

Instructions

In a bowl, combine the low-sodium soy sauce, rice vinegar, sesame oil, honey, and grated ginger to make the sauce.

In another bowl, toss the diced chicken with half of the sauce until well coated.

Place the chicken mixture on lettuce leaves.

Top with shredded carrots, chopped cucumber, and sesame seeds.

Drizzle the remaining sauce over the wraps.

Serve the Asian-inspired chicken lettuce wraps.

Enjoy!

Mediterranean Chickpea Salad:

Ingredients

1 cup canned chickpeas, rinsed and drained

½ cup diced cucumber

½ cup diced tomatoes

¼ cup diced red onion

¼ cup chopped Kalamata olives

2 tablespoons crumbled feta cheese

1 tablespoon extra-virgin olive oil

1 tablespoon lemon juice

1 tablespoon chopped fresh parsley

Salt and pepper to taste

Instructions

In a bowl, combine the chickpeas, cucumber, tomatoes, red onion, Kalamata olives, and crumbled feta cheese.

Drizzle with extra-virgin olive oil and lemon juice.

Sprinkle with chopped fresh parsley.

Season with salt and pepper to taste.

Toss gently to combine all the ingredients.

Serve the Mediterranean chickpea salad.

Enjoy!

Baked Salmon with Roasted Vegetables:

Ingredients

4 ounces (113 grams) salmon fillet

½ cup broccoli florets

½ cup cauliflower florets

½ cup sliced bell peppers

1 tablespoon olive oil

1 teaspoon lemon juice

1 teaspoon dried dill

Salt and pepper to taste

Instructions

Preheat the oven to 400°F (200°C).

Place the salmon fillet on a baking sheet lined with parchment paper.

In a separate bowl, toss the broccoli florets, cauliflower florets, and sliced bell peppers with olive oil, lemon juice, dried dill, salt, and pepper.

Spread the seasoned vegetables around the salmon on the baking sheet.

Bake for 12-15 minutes or until the salmon is cooked through and the vegetables are tender.

Serve the baked salmon with roasted vegetables.

Enjoy!

DINNER RECIPES FOR WEIGHT LOSS

Grilled Chicken Breast with Steamed Vegetables:

Ingredients

4 boneless, skinless chicken breasts

Salt and pepper to taste

1 tablespoon olive oil

Assorted steamed vegetables of your choice

Instructions

Preheat the grill to medium-high heat.

Season the chicken breasts with salt and pepper.

Brush the chicken breasts with olive oil.

Grill the chicken breasts for about 6-8 minutes per side, or until cooked through.

Meanwhile, steam your choice of vegetables until tender.

Serve the grilled chicken with the steamed vegetables.

Baked Salmon with Roasted Asparagus:

Ingredients

4 salmon fillets

Salt and pepper to taste

1 tablespoon olive oil

1 bunch asparagus, trimmed

Lemon wedges for serving

Instructions

Preheat the oven to 400°F (200°C).

Season the salmon fillets with salt and pepper.

Place the salmon fillets on a baking sheet lined with parchment paper.

Drizzle olive oil over the salmon fillets.

Arrange the asparagus alongside the salmon.

Season the asparagus with salt and pepper.

Bake for about 12-15 minutes or until the salmon is cooked through and the asparagus is tender.

Serve the baked salmon with roasted asparagus and lemon wedges.

Turkey Meatballs with Zucchini Noodles and Marinara Sauce:

Ingredients

1 pound ground turkey

1/4 cup whole wheat breadcrumbs

1/4 cup grated Parmesan cheese

1/4 cup finely chopped onion

2 cloves garlic, minced

1 egg, lightly beaten

Salt and pepper to taste

2 large zucchini, spiralized

2 cups marinara sauce

Instructions

Preheat the oven to 375°F (190°C).

In a large bowl, combine ground turkey, breadcrumbs, Parmesan cheese, onion, garlic, egg, salt, and pepper. Mix well.

Shape the mixture into meatballs of desired size.

Place the meatballs on a baking sheet lined with parchment paper.

Bake for about 20-25 minutes or until cooked through.

While the meatballs are baking, spiralize the zucchini into noodles using a spiralizer.

In a separate pan, heat the marinara sauce over medium heat.

Add the zucchini noodles to the marinara sauce and cook for a few minutes until heated through.

Serve the turkey meatballs with zucchini noodles and marinara sauce.

Baked Cod with Quinoa and Mixed Greens:

Ingredients

4 cod fillets

Salt and pepper to taste

1 tablespoon olive oil

1 cup cooked quinoa

Mixed greens for serving

Lemon wedges for serving

Instructions

Preheat the oven to 400°F (200°C).

Season the cod fillets with salt and pepper.

Place the cod fillets on a baking sheet lined with parchment paper.

Drizzle olive oil over the cod fillets.

Bake for about 12-15 minutes or until the cod is cooked through and flakes easily with a fork.

While the cod is baking, prepare the quinoa according to package instructions.

Serve the baked cod with a side of cooked quinoa and mixed greens.

Squeeze fresh lemon juice over the fish before serving.

Stir-Fried Tofu and Vegetables with Brown Rice:

Ingredients

1 tablespoon sesame oil

14 ounces (400g) firm tofu, drained and cubed

1 cup sliced mixed vegetables (such as bell peppers, broccoli, carrots)

2 cloves garlic, minced

2 tablespoons low-sodium soy sauce

1 tablespoon rice vinegar

2 cups cooked brown rice

Chopped green onions for garnish

Instructions

Heat sesame oil in a large skillet or wok over medium heat.

Add the tofu cubes to the skillet and cook until lightly browned on all sides.

Remove the tofu from the skillet and set aside.

In the same skillet, add the mixed vegetables and minced garlic. Stir-fry for a few minutes until the vegetables are crisp-tender.

In a small bowl, whisk together the soy sauce and rice vinegar. Pour the sauce over the vegetables in the skillet.

Return the tofu to the skillet and stir-fry for another minute or two to coat everything in the sauce.

Serve the stir-fried tofu and vegetables over cooked brown rice.

Garnish with chopped green onions.

Grilled Shrimp Skewers with Spinach Salad:

Ingredients

1 pound shrimp, peeled and deveined

Salt and pepper to taste

1 tablespoon olive oil

4 cups baby spinach

1 cup cherry tomatoes, halved

1/4 red onion, thinly sliced

2 tablespoons lemon juice

1 tablespoon balsamic vinegar

Instructions

Preheat the grill to medium-high heat.

Season the shrimp with salt, pepper, and olive oil.

Thread the shrimp onto skewers.

Grill the shrimp skewers for about 2-3 minutes per side, or until cooked through.

In a large bowl, combine baby spinach, cherry tomatoes, and red onion.

In a small bowl, whisk together lemon juice and balsamic vinegar to make the dressing.

Drizzle the dressing over the spinach salad and toss to coat.

Serve the grilled shrimp skewers alongside the spinach salad.

Baked Chicken Breast with Roasted Brussels Sprouts:

Ingredients

4 boneless, skinless chicken breasts

Salt and pepper to taste

1 tablespoon olive oil

1 pound Brussels sprouts, trimmed and halved

2 tablespoons balsamic vinegar

Instructions

Preheat the oven to 425°F (220°C).

Season the chicken breasts with salt and pepper.

Place the chicken breasts on a baking sheet lined with parchment paper.

Drizzle olive oil over the chicken breasts.

Bake for about 20-25 minutes or until the chicken is cooked through and no longer pink in the center.

While the chicken is baking, place the Brussels sprouts on a separate baking sheet.

Drizzle balsamic vinegar over the Brussels sprouts.

Roast the Brussels sprouts in the oven for about 15-20 minutes or until they are tender and lightly browned.

Serve the baked chicken breast with roasted Brussels sprouts.

Egg White Omelet with Mushrooms, Spinach, and Tomatoes:

Ingredients

Cooking spray

4 egg whites

Salt and pepper to taste

1/4 cup sliced mushrooms

1 cup fresh spinach

1/4 cup diced tomatoes

2 tablespoons grated Parmesan cheese

Instructions

Coat a non-stick skillet with cooking spray and heat over medium heat.

In a bowl, whisk the egg whites together with salt and pepper.

Pour the egg whites into the skillet and let them cook for a minute or two until the edges start to set.

Add the mushrooms, spinach, and tomatoes to one side of the omelet.

Sprinkle the Parmesan cheese over the vegetables.

Fold the other side of the omelet over the filling.

Cook for another minute or until the cheese is melted and the omelet is cooked through.

Slide the omelet onto a plate and serve.

Baked Tilapia with Steamed Broccoli and Wild Rice:

Ingredients

4 tilapia fillets

Salt and pepper to taste

1 tablespoon olive oil

1 pound broccoli florets

1 cup cooked wild rice

Instructions

Preheat the oven to 400°F (200°C).

Season the tilapia fillets with salt and pepper.

Place the tilapia fillets on a baking sheet lined with parchment paper.

Drizzle olive oil over the tilapia fillets.

Bake for about 12-15 minutes or until the fish is cooked through and flakes easily with a fork.

While the tilapia is baking, steam the broccoli until tender.

Serve the baked tilapia with a side of steamed broccoli and cooked wild rice.

Quinoa-Stuffed Bell Peppers with Mixed Greens:

Ingredients

4 bell peppers (any color)

1 cup cooked quinoa

1/2 cup canned black beans, rinsed and drained

1/2 cup diced tomatoes

1/4 cup diced red onion

1/4 cup corn kernels

1/4 cup chopped fresh cilantro

Salt and pepper to taste

Mixed greens for serving

Instructions

Preheat the oven to 375°F (190°C).

Cut the tops off the bell peppers and remove the seeds and membranes.

In a bowl, combine cooked quinoa, black beans, diced tomatoes, red onion, corn kernels, and cilantro.

Season the mixture with salt and pepper.

Spoon the quinoa mixture into the bell peppers.

Place the stuffed bell peppers in a baking dish.

Bake for about 25-30 minutes or until the peppers are tender and the filling is heated through.

Serve the quinoa-stuffed bell peppers with a side of mixed greens.

Turkey Chili with Kidney Beans and Diced Vegetables:

Ingredients

1 pound lean ground turkey

1 tablespoon olive oil

1 onion, diced

2 cloves garlic, minced

1 bell pepper, diced

1 zucchini, diced

1 can (14 ounces) diced tomatoes

1 can (14 ounces) kidney beans, rinsed and drained

1 tablespoon chili powder

1 teaspoon cumin

Salt and pepper to taste

Optional toppings: shredded cheese, chopped green onions, Greek yogurt

Instructions

In a large pot or Dutch oven, heat olive oil over medium heat.

Add the ground turkey and cook until browned.

Add the diced onion, minced garlic, bell pepper, and zucchini. Cook until the vegetables are softened.

Stir in the diced tomatoes, kidney beans, chili powder, cumin, salt, and pepper.

Bring the mixture to a boil, then reduce the heat and let it simmer for about 20-25 minutes.

Serve the turkey chili hot with optional toppings as desired.

Grilled Vegetable Skewers with Whole Wheat Couscous:

Ingredients

Assorted vegetables (such as bell peppers, zucchini, eggplant, cherry tomatoes, red onion), cut into chunks

2 tablespoons olive oil

2 tablespoons balsamic vinegar

1 teaspoon dried herbs (such as oregano, basil, thyme)

Salt and pepper to taste

1 cup whole wheat couscous

Fresh parsley for garnish

Instructions

Preheat the grill to medium-high heat.

In a bowl, combine the vegetables, olive oil, balsamic vinegar, dried herbs, salt, and pepper. Toss to coat the vegetables evenly.

Thread the vegetables onto skewers.

Grill the vegetable skewers for about 10-12 minutes, turning occasionally, until they are charred and tender.

While the vegetables are grilling, prepare the whole wheat couscous according to the package instructions.

Serve the grilled vegetable skewers over a bed of whole wheat couscous. Garnish with fresh parsley.

Baked Lean Steak with Grilled Asparagus:

Ingredients

4 lean steak cuts (such as sirloin, flank, or tenderloin)

Salt and pepper to taste

1 tablespoon olive oil

1 bunch asparagus, trimmed

Optional: minced garlic or lemon zest for additional flavor

Instructions

Preheat the oven to 425°F (220°C).

Season the steak cuts with salt and pepper.

Heat olive oil in an oven-safe skillet over high heat.

Sear the steaks for about 2 minutes per side to form a crust.

Transfer the skillet to the preheated oven and bake for about 8-10 minutes for medium-rare, or longer to desired doneness.

While the steak is baking, toss the trimmed asparagus with olive oil, salt, pepper, and any additional flavorings, if desired.

Grill the asparagus over medium-high heat for about 4-6 minutes, turning occasionally, until it is tender-crisp and charred in spots.

Let the steak rest for a few minutes before slicing.

Serve the baked lean steak with grilled asparagus.

Spaghetti Squash with Turkey Bolognese Sauce:

Ingredients

1 medium spaghetti squash

1 tablespoon olive oil

1 pound ground turkey

1 onion, diced

2 cloves garlic, minced

1 carrot, diced

1 stalk celery, diced

1 can (14 ounces) diced tomatoes

1 can (6 ounces) tomato paste

1 teaspoon dried basil

1 teaspoon dried oregano

Salt and pepper to taste

Fresh basil for garnish

Instructions

Preheat the oven to 400°F (200°C).

Cut the spaghetti squash in half lengthwise and scoop out the seeds.

Drizzle the cut sides of the squash with olive oil and season with salt and pepper.

Place the squash halves cut-side down on a baking sheet.

Bake for about 40-50 minutes or until the squash flesh is tender and easily pulls apart into strands with a fork.

While the squash is baking, prepare the turkey Bolognese sauce. In a large skillet, heat olive oil over medium heat.

Add the ground turkey and cook until browned.

Add the diced onion, minced garlic, carrot, and celery. Cook until the vegetables are softened.

Stir in the diced tomatoes, tomato paste, dried basil, dried oregano, salt, and pepper. Simmer for about 15-20 minutes to let the flavors meld.

Use a fork to scrape the cooked spaghetti squash flesh into strands.

Serve the spaghetti squash topped with the turkey Bolognese sauce. Garnish with fresh basil.

Lentil Soup with Mixed Green Salad:

Ingredients

1 tablespoon olive oil

1 onion, diced

2 carrots, diced

2 stalks celery, diced

2 cloves garlic, minced

1 cup dried lentils, rinsed and drained

4 cups low-sodium vegetable or chicken broth

2 cups water

1 bay leaf

1 teaspoon dried thyme

Salt and pepper to taste

Mixed greens for salad

Dressing of your choice

Instructions

In a large pot, heat olive oil over medium heat.

Add the diced onion, carrots, celery, and minced garlic. Sauté until the vegetables are softened.

Add the dried lentils, vegetable or chicken broth, water, bay leaf, dried thyme, salt, and pepper to the pot.

Bring the mixture to a boil, then reduce the heat and let it simmer for about 30-40 minutes or until the lentils are tender.

Remove the bay leaf before serving.

While the soup is simmering, prepare a mixed green salad by combining your choice of greens and topping it with your preferred dressing.

Serve the lentil soup with a side of mixed green salad.

Grilled Tofu with Roasted Sweet Potatoes:

Ingredients

1 block (14-16 ounces) extra-firm tofu

1/4 cup low-sodium soy sauce

2 tablespoons maple syrup

1 tablespoon rice vinegar

1 tablespoon sesame oil

2 sweet potatoes, peeled and cut into cubes

1 tablespoon olive oil

Salt and pepper to taste

Fresh cilantro for garnish

Instructions

Press the tofu to remove excess moisture. Cut the tofu into cubes.

In a bowl, whisk together soy sauce, maple syrup, rice vinegar, and sesame oil.

Add the tofu cubes to the marinade, making sure they are well-coated. Let them marinate for at least 30 minutes, or longer if possible.

Preheat the grill to medium-high heat.

Thread the tofu cubes onto skewers.

Grill the tofu skewers for about 2-3 minutes per side until they are lightly charred and heated through.

While the tofu is grilling, toss the sweet potato cubes with olive oil, salt, and pepper. Spread them out on a baking sheet.

Roast the sweet potatoes in the oven at 425°F (220°C) for about 25-30 minutes or until they are tender and golden.

Serve the grilled tofu skewers with roasted sweet potatoes. Garnish with fresh cilantro.

Lemon Herb Grilled Chicken with Steamed Green Beans:

Ingredients

4 boneless, skinless chicken breasts

Juice of 2 lemons

Zest of 1 lemon

2 tablespoons olive oil

2 cloves garlic, minced

1 teaspoon dried thyme

Salt and pepper to taste

1 pound green beans, trimmed

Instructions

In a bowl, combine the lemon juice, lemon zest, olive oil, minced garlic, dried thyme, salt, and pepper.

Place the chicken breasts in a shallow dish and pour the marinade over them. Let them marinate for at least 30 minutes, or longer if possible.

Preheat the grill to medium-high heat.

Grill the chicken breasts for about 6-8 minutes per side, or until they are cooked through and reach an internal temperature of 165°F (74°C).

While the chicken is grilling, steam the green beans until they are tender-crisp.

Serve the grilled lemon herb chicken with steamed green beans.

Veggie Stir-Fry with Brown Rice:

Ingredients

1 tablespoon sesame oil

1 onion, thinly sliced

2 cloves garlic, minced

1 bell pepper, thinly sliced

1 zucchini, thinly sliced

1 cup sliced mushrooms

1 cup broccoli florets

1 carrot, thinly sliced

2 tablespoons low-sodium soy sauce

1 tablespoon rice vinegar

1 tablespoon honey or maple syrup

2 cups cooked brown rice

Instructions

Heat sesame oil in a large skillet or wok over medium heat.

Add the sliced onion and minced garlic. Sauté for a few minutes until they are softened and fragrant.

Add the bell pepper, zucchini, mushrooms, broccoli florets, and carrot to the skillet. Stir-fry for about 5-7 minutes or until the vegetables are tender-crisp.

In a small bowl, whisk together the soy sauce, rice vinegar, and honey or maple syrup to make the sauce.

Pour the sauce over the vegetables in the skillet and toss to coat everything evenly.

Cook for another minute or two to heat the sauce.

Serve the veggie stir-fry over cooked brown rice.

Grilled Salmon with Quinoa and Roasted Vegetables:

Ingredients

4 salmon fillets

Salt and pepper to taste

1 tablespoon olive oil

1 cup cooked quinoa

Assorted roasted vegetables (such as carrots, Brussels sprouts, and cauliflower)

Lemon wedges for serving

Instructions

Preheat the grill to medium-high heat.

Season the salmon fillets with salt and pepper.

Drizzle olive oil over the salmon fillets.

Grill the salmon for about 4-5 minutes per side, or until it is cooked through and flakes easily with a fork.

While the salmon is grilling, prepare the quinoa according to package instructions.

Roast the vegetables in the oven until they are tender and lightly browned.

Serve the grilled salmon with a side of cooked quinoa and roasted vegetables.

Squeeze fresh lemon juice over the salmon before serving.

Quinoa and Black Bean Stuffed Bell Peppers:

Ingredients

4 bell peppers (any color)

1 cup cooked quinoa

1 can (14 ounces) black beans, rinsed and drained

1 cup diced tomatoes

1/4 cup diced red onion

1/4 cup corn kernels

1/4 cup chopped fresh cilantro

1 teaspoon cumin

1/2 teaspoon chili powder

Salt and pepper to taste

Optional toppings: shredded cheese, Greek yogurt, salsa

Instructions

Preheat the oven to 375°F (190°C).

Cut the tops off the bell peppers and remove the seeds and membranes.

In a bowl, combine the cooked quinoa, black beans, diced tomatoes, red onion, corn kernels, chopped cilantro, cumin, chili powder, salt, and pepper. Stir to mix everything well.

Stuff the bell peppers with the quinoa and black bean mixture.

Place the stuffed bell peppers in a baking dish.

Bake for about 25-30 minutes or until the peppers are tender and the filling is heated through.

Serve the quinoa and black bean stuffed bell peppers with optional toppings as desired.

SOUP RECIPES FOR WEIGHT LOSS

Vegetable Soup:

Ingredients

Assorted vegetables (carrots, broccoli, bell peppers, zucchini, etc.)

Vegetable broth

Garlic, onion, herbs (such as thyme or basil)

Salt and pepper.

Instructions

Chop the vegetables into bite-sized pieces.

In a large pot, sauté the garlic and onion until fragrant.

Add the chopped vegetables and cook for a few minutes.

Pour in enough vegetable broth to cover the vegetables and bring to a boil.

Reduce the heat and simmer until the vegetables are tender.

Season with herbs, salt, and pepper to taste.

Serve hot.

Lentil Soup:

Ingredients

Lentils

Vegetable broth

Assorted vegetables (carrots, celery, onions, etc.)

Garlic, cumin, paprika

Salt and pepper.

Instructions

Rinse the lentils and set aside.

In a large pot, sauté the garlic, onions, and vegetables until softened.

Add the lentils and vegetable broth to the pot.

Bring to a boil, then reduce heat and simmer until the lentils are tender.

Season with cumin, paprika, salt, and pepper.

Cook for another few minutes and serve hot.

Chicken and Vegetable Soup:

Ingredients

Chicken breast (skinless and boneless)

Low-sodium chicken broth

Assorted vegetables (carrots, celery, onions, etc.)

Garlic, thyme, rosemary

Salt and pepper.

Instructions

Cut the chicken breast into small pieces.

In a large pot, sauté the garlic, onions, and vegetables until slightly softened.

Add the chicken pieces and cook until no longer pink.

Pour in the chicken broth and bring to a boil.

Reduce heat and simmer until the chicken is cooked through and the vegetables are tender.

Season with thyme, rosemary, salt, and pepper.

Allow it to simmer for a few more minutes and serve hot.

Minestrone Soup:

Ingredients

Low-sodium vegetable broth

Canned diced tomatoes

Kidney beans

Whole wheat pasta (small shapes like macaroni or shells)

Assorted vegetables (carrots, celery, zucchini, green beans, etc.)

Garlic, onion, basil, oregano

Salt and pepper.

Instructions

In a large pot, sauté the garlic and onion until fragrant.

Add the vegetables and cook for a few minutes.

Pour in the vegetable broth and diced tomatoes (with their juice).

Bring to a boil and then add the kidney beans.

Reduce the heat and simmer until the vegetables are tender.

Cook the whole wheat pasta separately according to the package instructions and add it to the pot.

Season with basil, oregano, salt, and pepper.

Simmer for a few more minutes and serve hot.

Tomato Basil Soup:

Ingredients

Canned crushed tomatoes

Vegetable broth

Onion, garlic

Fresh basil, dried thyme, olive oil

Salt and pepper.

Instructions

In a large pot, sauté the onion and garlic in olive oil until softened.

Add the crushed tomatoes and vegetable broth.

Bring to a boil, then reduce heat and simmer for about 15-20 minutes.

Stir in the fresh basil and dried thyme.

Season with salt and pepper to taste.

Simmer for a few more minutes and serve hot.

Cabbage Soup:

Ingredients

Cabbage

Onions

Celery

Carrots

Vegetable broth

Garlic, paprika, bay leaves

Salt and pepper.

Instructions

Chop the cabbage, onions, celery, and carrots into bite-sized pieces.

In a large pot, sauté the garlic until fragrant.

Add the onions, celery, and carrots to the pot and cook until slightly softened.

Stir in the cabbage and cook for a few minutes.

Pour in the vegetable broth, add bay leaves, and bring to a boil.

Reduce heat and simmer until the vegetables are tender.

Season with paprika, salt, and pepper.

Cook for another few minutes and serve hot.

Black Bean Soup:

Ingredients

Black beans (canned or cooked from dried)

Vegetable broth

Onion, garlic, cumin, chili powder

Lime juice

Cilantro

Salt and pepper.

Instructions

In a blender or food processor, blend half of the black beans with a little vegetable broth until smooth.

In a large pot, sauté the onion and garlic until softened.

Add the blended beans, remaining whole beans, and vegetable broth to the pot.

Stir in cumin, chili powder, lime juice, cilantro, salt, and pepper.

Bring to a simmer and cook for about 15-20 minutes.

Adjust the seasoning if needed.

Serve hot.

Gazpacho:

Ingredients

Ripe tomatoes

Cucumbers

Bell peppers, red onion, garlic, tomato juice

Olive oil

Red wine vinegar

Salt and pepper

Optional toppings (diced cucumber, red onion, croutons).

Instructions

Chop the tomatoes, cucumbers, bell peppers, and red onion into small pieces.

In a blender or food processor, blend half of the chopped vegetables with garlic, tomato juice, olive oil, and red wine vinegar until smooth.

Pour the blended mixture into a large bowl and stir in the remaining chopped vegetables.

Season with salt and pepper.

Cover and refrigerate for a few hours to allow the flavors to meld.

Serve chilled with optional toppings.

Broccoli Soup:

Ingredients

Broccoli florets

Low-fat milk or non-dairy alternative

Vegetable broth

Onion, garlic, nutmeg

Salt and pepper.

Instructions

Steam or boil the broccoli florets until tender.

In a large pot, sauté the onion and garlic until softened.

Add the steamed broccoli, vegetable broth, and low-fat milk (or non-dairy alternative) to the pot.

Bring to a simmer and cook for about 10 minutes.

Use an immersion blender or transfer the mixture to a blender to puree until smooth.

Season with nutmeg, salt, and pepper.

Simmer for a few more minutes and serve hot.

Spinach Soup:

Ingredients

Fresh spinach leaves

Vegetable broth

Onion, garlic

Low-fat milk or non-dairy alternative

Nutmeg

Salt and pepper.

Instructions

In a large pot, sauté the onion and garlic until softened.

Add the spinach leaves and cook until wilted.

Pour in the vegetable broth and bring to a boil.

Reduce heat and simmer for about 10 minutes.

Use an immersion blender or transfer the mixture to a blender to puree until smooth.

Stir in the low-fat milk or non-dairy alternative.

Season with nutmeg, salt, and pepper.

Simmer for a few more minutes and serve hot.

Carrot Ginger Soup:

Ingredients

Carrots

Ginger

Vegetable broth

Onion, garlic, turmeric, cumin, coriander

Salt and pepper.

Instructions

Peel and chop the carrots into small pieces.

In a large pot, sauté the onion, garlic, and ginger until fragrant.

Add the chopped carrots and cook for a few minutes.

Pour in the vegetable broth and bring to a boil.

Reduce heat and simmer until the carrots are tender.

Use an immersion blender or transfer the mixture to a blender to puree until smooth.

Season with turmeric, cumin, coriander, salt, and pepper.

Simmer for a few more minutes and serve hot.

Mushroom Soup:

Ingredients

Assorted mushrooms (such as cremini, button, or shiitake)

Vegetable broth

Onion, garlic, thyme

Low-fat milk or non-dairy alternative

Salt and pepper.

Instructions

Clean and slice the mushrooms.

In a large pot, sauté the onion, garlic, and mushrooms until softened.

Add the vegetable broth and bring to a boil.

Reduce heat and simmer for about 15 minutes.

Use an immersion blender or transfer the mixture to a blender to puree until smooth.

Stir in the low-fat milk or non-dairy alternative.

Season with thyme, salt, and pepper.

Simmer for a few more minutes and serve hot.

Cauliflower Soup:

Ingredients

Cauliflower

Vegetable broth

Onion, garlic

Low-fat milk or non-dairy alternative

Thyme, paprika

Salt and pepper.

Instructions

Cut the cauliflower into florets.

In a large pot, sauté the onion and garlic until softened.

Add the cauliflower and vegetable broth to the pot.

Bring to a boil, then reduce heat and simmer until the cauliflower is tender.

Use an immersion blender or transfer the mixture to a blender to puree until smooth.

Stir in the low-fat milk or non-dairy alternative.

Season with thyme, paprika, salt, and pepper.

Simmer for a few more minutes and serve hot.

Thai Coconut Soup:

Ingredients

Coconut milk

Vegetable broth

Mushrooms, bell peppers, lemongrass

Ginger, garlic

Lime juice

Soy sauce or tamari

Chili paste

Cilantro

Salt and pepper.

Instructions

Slice the mushrooms and bell peppers.

In a large pot, combine the coconut milk and vegetable broth.

Add the mushrooms, bell peppers, lemongrass, ginger, and garlic.

Bring to a boil, then reduce heat and simmer for about 10 minutes.

Stir in lime juice, soy sauce or tamari, and chili paste.

Season with cilantro, salt, and pepper.

Simmer for a few more minutes and serve hot.

Chicken Tortilla Soup:

Ingredients

Chicken breast (skinless and boneless)

Low-sodium chicken broth

Canned diced tomatoes

Corn

Black beans

Onion, garlic, cumin, chili powder

Lime juice, cilantro

Salt and pepper.

Instructions

Cut the chicken breast into small pieces.

In a large pot, sauté the onion and garlic until softened.

Add the chicken pieces and cook until no longer pink.

Pour in the chicken broth and bring to a boil.

Add the diced tomatoes, corn, and black beans to the pot.

Stir in cumin, chili powder, lime juice, cilantro, salt, and pepper.

Simmer for about 20-25 minutes until flavors are well combined.

Adjust the seasoning if needed.

Serve hot, and you can garnish with tortilla strips if desired.

Egg Drop Soup:

Ingredients

Low-sodium chicken or vegetable broth

Eggs

Green onions (scallions)

Soy sauce or tamari

Sesame oil

Salt and pepper.

Instructions

In a saucepan, bring the chicken or vegetable broth to a simmer.

Beat the eggs in a small bowl.

Slowly pour the beaten eggs into the simmering broth while stirring gently with a fork to create delicate egg ribbons.

Add thinly sliced green onions (scallions).

Season with soy sauce or tamari, sesame oil, salt, and pepper to taste.

Simmer for a few more minutes and serve hot.

Sweet Potato Soup:

Ingredients

Sweet potatoes

Vegetable broth

Onion, garlic, ground cinnamon, ground nutmeg

Low-fat milk or non-dairy alternative

Salt and pepper.

Instructions

Peel and dice the sweet potatoes.

In a large pot, sauté the onion and garlic until softened.

Add the diced sweet potatoes and vegetable broth to the pot.

Bring to a boil, then reduce heat and simmer until the sweet potatoes are tender.

Use an immersion blender or transfer the mixture to a blender to puree until smooth.

Stir in the low-fat milk or non-dairy alternative.

Season with ground cinnamon, ground nutmeg, salt, and pepper.

Simmer for a few more minutes and serve hot.

Butternut Squash Soup:

Ingredients

Butternut squash

Vegetable broth

Onion, garlic, ground ginger, ground cinnamon

Low-fat milk or non-dairy alternative

Salt and pepper.

Instructions

Peel, seed, and chop the butternut squash.

In a large pot, sauté the onion and garlic until softened.

Add the chopped butternut squash and vegetable broth to the pot.

Bring to a boil, then reduce heat and simmer until the butternut squash is tender.

Use an immersion blender or transfer the mixture to a blender to puree until smooth.

Stir in the low-fat milk or non-dairy alternative.

Season with ground ginger, ground cinnamon, salt, and pepper.

Simmer for a few more minutes and serve hot.

Split Pea Soup:

Ingredients

Dried split peas

Vegetable broth

Onion, garlic

Carrots

Celery

Bay leaf, dried thyme

Salt and pepper.

Instructions

Rinse the split peas and set aside.

In a large pot, sauté the onion and garlic until softened.

Add the split peas, vegetable broth, and bay leaf to the pot.

Bring to a boil, then reduce heat and simmer for about 30-40 minutes until the split peas are tender and the soup thickens.

Stir in the diced carrots and celery.

Season with dried thyme, salt, and pepper.

Simmer for a few more minutes and serve hot.

Fish Chowder:

Ingredients

White fish fillets (such as cod or tilapia)

Potatoes

Vegetable broth

Onion, garlic

Low-fat milk or non-dairy alternative

Thyme

Salt and pepper.

Instructions

Cut the white fish fillets into bite-sized pieces.

Peel and dice the potatoes.

In a large pot, sauté the onion and garlic until softened.

Add the diced potatoes and vegetable broth to the pot.

Bring to a boil, then reduce heat and simmer until the potatoes are tender.

Stir in the fish pieces and cook until they are cooked through and flaky.

Pour in the low-fat milk or non-dairy alternative.

Season with thyme, salt, and pepper.

Simmer for a few more minutes and serve hot.

DESSERT RECIPES FOR WEIGHT LOSS

Baked Apples:

Ingredients

Apples (any variety)

Cinnamon (optional)

Instructions

Preheat the oven to 375°F (190°C).

Core the apples and place them in a baking dish.

Sprinkle cinnamon over the apples if desired.

Bake for 20-25 minutes or until the apples are tender.

Serve warm.

Greek Yogurt Parfait:

Ingredients

Greek yogurt (unsweetened)

Mixed berries (such as strawberries, blueberries, raspberries)

Granola (low-sugar or homemade)

Instructions

In a glass or bowl, layer Greek yogurt, mixed berries, and a small amount of granola.

Repeat the layers until desired.

Enjoy immediately.

Chia Seed Pudding:

Ingredients

Chia seeds

Unsweetened almond milk (or any non-dairy milk)

Natural sweetener (such as honey or maple syrup)

Instructions

In a bowl or jar, combine 2 tablespoons of chia seeds with 1/2 cup of almond milk.

Add a natural sweetener to taste and mix well.

Let the mixture sit for about 5 minutes and then stir again.

Cover and refrigerate overnight or for at least 2 hours until the pudding thickens.

Serve chilled.

Frozen Grapes:

Ingredients

Grapes (any variety)

Instructions

Rinse the grapes and pat them dry.

Place the grapes in a single layer on a baking sheet or tray.

Freeze the grapes for at least 2 hours or until firm.

Serve the frozen grapes as a refreshing snack.

Fruit Salad:

Ingredients

Assorted fresh fruits (such as berries, melons, oranges, kiwis, grapes)

Instructions

Wash, peel, and chop the fruits into bite-sized pieces.

Combine the fruits in a bowl and gently toss.

Serve the fruit salad chilled.

Berry Smoothie:

Ingredients

Mixed berries (such as strawberries, blueberries, raspberries)

Unsweetened almond milk (or any non-dairy milk)

Ice cubes

Instructions

In a blender, combine a handful of mixed berries, 1 cup of almond milk, and a few ice cubes.

Blend until smooth and creamy.

Pour into a glass and serve immediately.

Dark Chocolate:

Ingredients

High-quality dark chocolate (70% cocoa or higher)

Instructions

Break off a small piece of dark chocolate.

Enjoy it as is or savor it slowly.

Banana "Nice Cream":

Ingredients

Ripe bananas (peeled and frozen)

Instructions

Place frozen bananas in a blender or food processor.

Blend until smooth and creamy, scraping down the sides as needed.

Serve immediately as soft-serve ice cream or freeze for a firmer texture.

Baked Peaches:

Ingredients

Peaches (ripe but firm)

Cinnamon (optional)

Instructions

Preheat the oven to 375°F (190°C).

Slice the peaches in half and remove the pits.

Place the peaches on a baking sheet, cut side up.

Sprinkle cinnamon over the peaches if desired.

Bake for 15-20 minutes or until the peaches are tender.

Serve warm.

Rice Cake with Nut Butter:

Ingredients

Rice cakes (plain or lightly salted)

Natural nut butter (such as almond butter or peanut butter)

Instructions

Spread a thin layer of nut butter onto a rice cake.

Enjoy it as is or top with sliced fruit for added flavor.

Cottage Cheese with Berries:

Ingredients

Cottage cheese (low-fat or fat-free)

Mixed berries (such as strawberries, blueberries, raspberries)

Instructions

Place a serving of cottage cheese in a bowl.

Top with a handful of mixed berries.

Mix gently and enjoy.

Citrus Sorbet:

Ingredients

Freshly squeezed citrus juice (such as orange, grapefruit, or lemon)

Natural sweetener (optional)

Instructions

In a bowl, combine the citrus juice with a natural sweetener if desired.

Pour the mixture into an ice cream maker and follow the manufacturer's instructions.

Once the sorbet reaches the desired consistency, transfer it to a container and freeze for a couple of hours.

Serve chilled.

Almond Date Balls:

Ingredients

Dates (pitted)

Almonds

Instructions

Place dates and almonds in a food processor.

Process until the mixture comes together and forms a sticky dough.

Take small portions and roll the mixture into balls.

Place the balls in the refrigerator to firm up.

Enjoy chilled.

Watermelon Popsicles:

Ingredients

Watermelon chunks (seedless)

Popsicle molds

Instructions

Puree the watermelon chunks in a blender or food processor until smooth.

Pour the watermelon puree into popsicle molds.

Insert popsicle sticks and freeze until solid.

Remove the popsicles from the molds and enjoy.

Baked Pears:

Ingredients

Pears (firm)

Cinnamon (optional)

Instructions

Preheat the oven to 375°F (190°C).

Slice the pears into halves or quarters and remove the cores.

Place the pears on a baking sheet.

Sprinkle cinnamon over the pears if desired.

Bake for 20-25 minutes or until the pears are tender.

Serve warm.

Yogurt Bark:

Ingredients

Greek yogurt (unsweetened)

Mixed berries (such as strawberries, blueberries, raspberries)

Instructions

Line a baking sheet with parchment paper.

Spread a layer of Greek yogurt evenly on the parchment paper.

Scatter mixed berries on top of the yogurt.

Place the baking sheet in the freezer for a couple of hours or until the bark is firm.

Break the bark into pieces and enjoy.

Cinnamon Roasted Almonds:

Ingredients

Almonds

Cinnamon

Natural sweetener (such as honey or maple syrup, optional)

Instructions

Preheat the oven to 325°F (165°C).

In a bowl, toss the almonds with cinnamon and a natural sweetener if desired.

Spread the almonds on a baking sheet in a single layer.

Roast for about 15-20 minutes, stirring occasionally, until the almonds are fragrant and lightly browned.

Allow them to cool before enjoying.

Protein Pancakes:

Ingredients

Protein powder (of your choice)

Whole-grain pancake mix

Fresh fruit (optional, for topping)

Instructions

Prepare the pancake batter according to the instructions on the package.

Add a scoop of protein powder to the batter and mix well.

Cook the pancakes on a griddle or non-stick pan until golden brown.

Serve with fresh fruit on top, if desired.

Cocoa Roasted Chickpeas:

Ingredients

Canned chickpeas (drained and rinsed)

Unsweetened cocoa powder

Natural sweetener (such as honey or maple syrup, optional)

Instructions

Preheat the oven to 400°F (200°C).

In a bowl, combine the chickpeas, cocoa powder, and a natural sweetener if desired.

Spread the mixture on a baking sheet in a single layer.

Roast for about 25-30 minutes, stirring occasionally, until the chickpeas are crispy.

Allow them to cool before serving.

Apple Cinnamon Oatmeal Cookies:

Ingredients

Rolled oats

Applesauce (unsweetened)

Cinnamon

Natural sweetener (such as honey or maple syrup, optional)

Instructions

Preheat the oven to 350°F (175°C).

In a bowl, mix together rolled oats, applesauce, cinnamon, and a natural sweetener if desired.

Form the mixture into small cookie shapes and place them on a baking sheet lined with parchment paper.

Bake for 12-15 minutes or until the cookies are golden brown.

Allow them to cool before enjoying.

PART 4: ONE LAST THING BEFORE YOU GO

Overall, The Mayo Clinic Diet provides a methodical and scientifically-supported strategy for achieving weight loss and better health. It stresses lasting lifestyle improvements such healthy eating, portion control, frequent exercise, and modifying undesirable habits. Weight reduction is slow and sustainable when following the diet's recommendations, and there are other health advantages as well.

The Mayo Clinic Diet is unique because it tailors its recommendations to each individual's needs, tastes, and health status. Fruits, vegetables, whole grains, lean proteins, and healthy fats are advocated, whereas processed foods, added sugars, harmful fats, and salt are discouraged or limited.

The Mayo Clinic Diet is designed to do more than only promote weight reduction; it also prioritizes the well-being of its adherents. It helps people on their weight-loss journey by focusing on behavior modification to bring about long-term improvements in lifestyle.

To get individualized advice and make sure the diet is appropriate for one's requirements and health problems, however, it is best to speak with a certified dietitian or other healthcare expert.

In conclusion, The Mayo Clinic Diet is a reliable and efficient program that helps people lose weight and improve their health by teaching them how to make permanent adjustments in their eating and daily routines.

Maintaining Sustainable Weight Loss on The Mayo Clinic Diet

Sticking to the ideas and practices established in the beginning stages of The Mayo Clinic Diet is essential for long-term weight maintenance. Here are some of the most important things people can do to keep the weight off permanently:

Adopting healthy eating habits consistently is one of the cornerstones of The Mayo Clinic Diet. Fruits, vegetables, whole grains, lean meats, and healthy fats should all be part of every day's diet. Maintaining weight reduction and improving health requires a consistent commitment to eating a diet that is both balanced and healthy.

Mindful eating and portion management: portion control is an important factor in weight maintenance. Mindful eating can help you keep track of how much you're eating and prevent overeating. Listen to your body for signals of hunger and fullness, eat gently, and enjoy every meal. Being conscious of one's portion sizes is an important step in maintaining a balanced diet and a healthy perspective on food.

Maintaining a healthy weight and fitness level requires regular physical exercise. The Mayo Clinic Diet stresses the importance of maintaining an active lifestyle. Weight reduction and general fitness may be maintained with the use of activities that you love, such as walking, running, cycling, or strength training. Include strength training activities at least twice per week and aim for at least 150 minutes of moderate-intensity aerobic activity or 75 minutes of vigorous-intensity aerobic activity each week.

For lasting success, it's important to keep using the skills you learned in The Mayo Clinic Diet's behavior modification module. Maintaining weight reduction success and overcoming difficulties can be aided by strategies including identifying emotional eating triggers, creating healthy coping techniques, and setting realistic objectives.

Keeping a record of one's daily food consumption, level of physical activity, and progress may serve as a kind of accountability and help one see areas for growth. Self-monitoring on a regular basis, whether through food diaries, smartphone applications, or other tracking methods, helps individuals maintain awareness of their actions and make appropriate modifications.

Seek Out Encouragement and Expert Advice: Maintaining a healthy weight is much easier if you have someone to hold you accountable. It's a good idea to look into support groups, internet forums, and licensed nutritionists and doctors for advice. They can be there for you whenever you have questions or concerns, and they can help you figure out how to modify your diet to fit your ever-changing lifestyle.

By sticking to these methods and leading a healthy lifestyle, dieters on The Mayo Clinic Diet can shed pounds and feel better about their health for the long haul.

Incorporating Exercises

An integral part of losing weight and keeping it off while following The Mayo Clinic Diet is engaging in regular physical activity. If you want to include exercise into your diet successfully, you should stick to these recommendations.

The first step in selecting the best activities for you is taking stock of your current fitness level. Before beginning an exercise program, it's smart to check in with your doctor if you have any preexisting problems or worries.

Pick out some physical activities that you'll look forward to doing. If you do this, you'll have a better chance of maintaining your fitness regimen over time. Find anything you enjoy doing that gets you moving, whether it's a brisk walk, jog, bike ride, swim, dance, or group exercise class, and stick with it.

In order to shed pounds and get in shape, cardio is an absolute must. Aim for at least 75 minutes of strenuous aerobic activity each week, or 150 minutes of moderate aerobic activity. Walking, jogging, cycling, swimming, and aerobics classes all fit the bill. If you divide the time commitment into small weekly sessions, you'll be more likely to stick to the suggested schedule.

Building lean muscle mass, elevating your metabolism, and enhancing your overall body composition are all goals that may be achieved with regular strength training. Perform strength-training exercises at least twice a week, focusing on your legs, arms, chest, back, shoulders, and core. Squats, lunges, push-ups, and planks are just some of the workouts that may be performed using resistance bands, free weights, weight machines, or even just your own body weight.

Don't overlook the importance of flexibility and stretching exercises in fostering mobility and warding off injuries. You may stretch before, during, and after your workouts, or just on its own. Think about doing something like yoga or Pilates, which can help you get stronger, more flexible, and more in tune with yourself.

Increase the intensity of your workout regimen gradually. You should ease into your exercises and then progressively challenge yourself by increasing their duration, intensity, or both. This kind of training is safer and more effective since it allows the body to gradually adjust to new levels of exertion.

In addition, make it a priority to maintain physical exercise at regular intervals throughout the day. Engage in physically active pastimes like gardening or dancing, or just take little walks when you can. Consistently making these kinds of modest motions can help you burn more calories and encourage you to lead a more active lifestyle.

Always pay attention to your body, drink enough of water, and schedule rest days for effective recuperation. If you're not sure where to start or would like some individualized advice, a fitness expert or certified personal trainer may help you create an exercise plan that is specific to your requirements and objectives.

The weight reduction, fitness, and health benefits of The Mayo Clinic Diet can be maximized and sustained with consistent physical activity.

Made in the USA
Monee, IL
16 September 2023

42841342R10134